This Book Belongs To

_____

_____

Copyright 2022 Acts 10.1 BookS
Jobos101 is Trademarked by: Jahlyric Boldini Designs, Llc
www.Jobos101.com

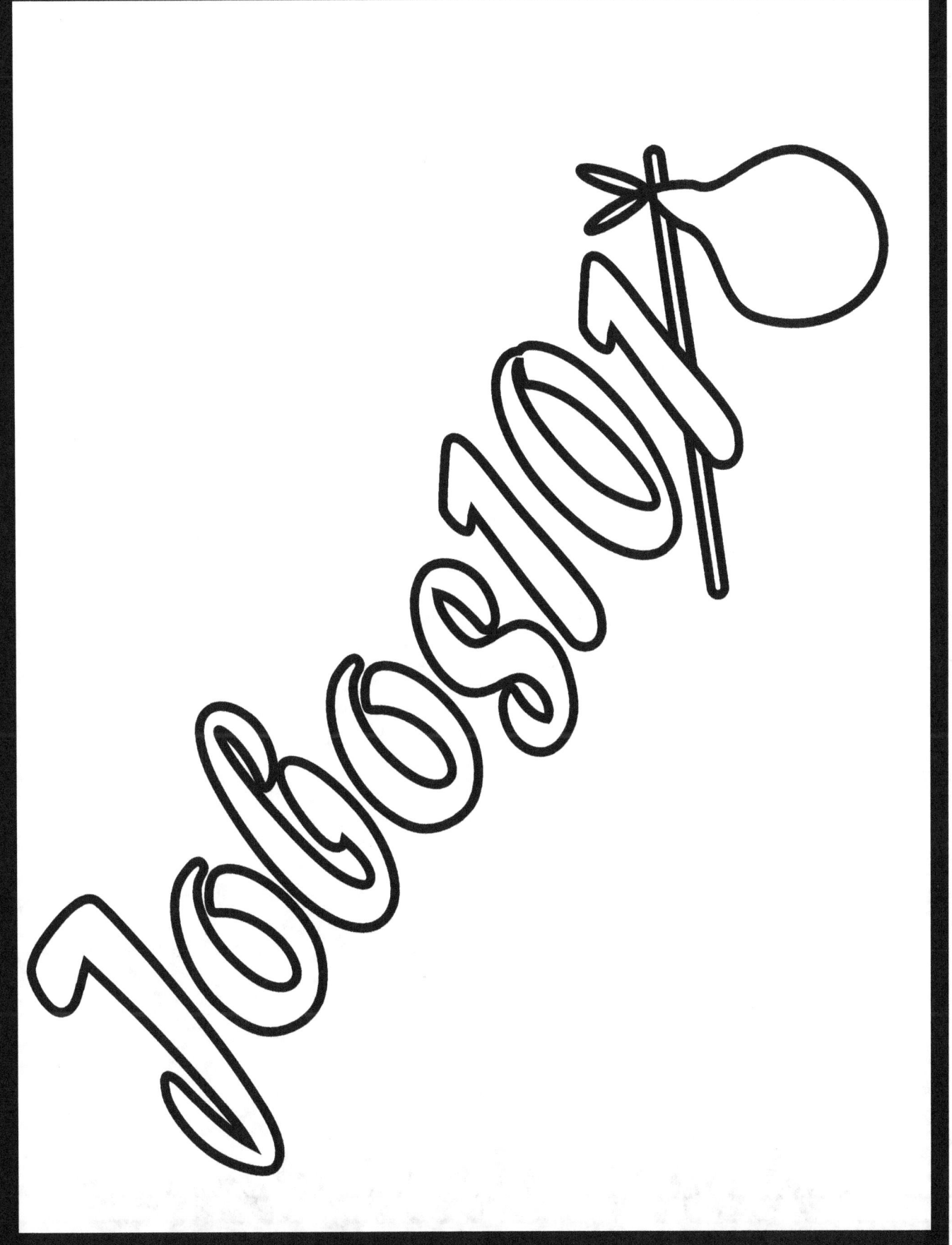

Merry Christmas

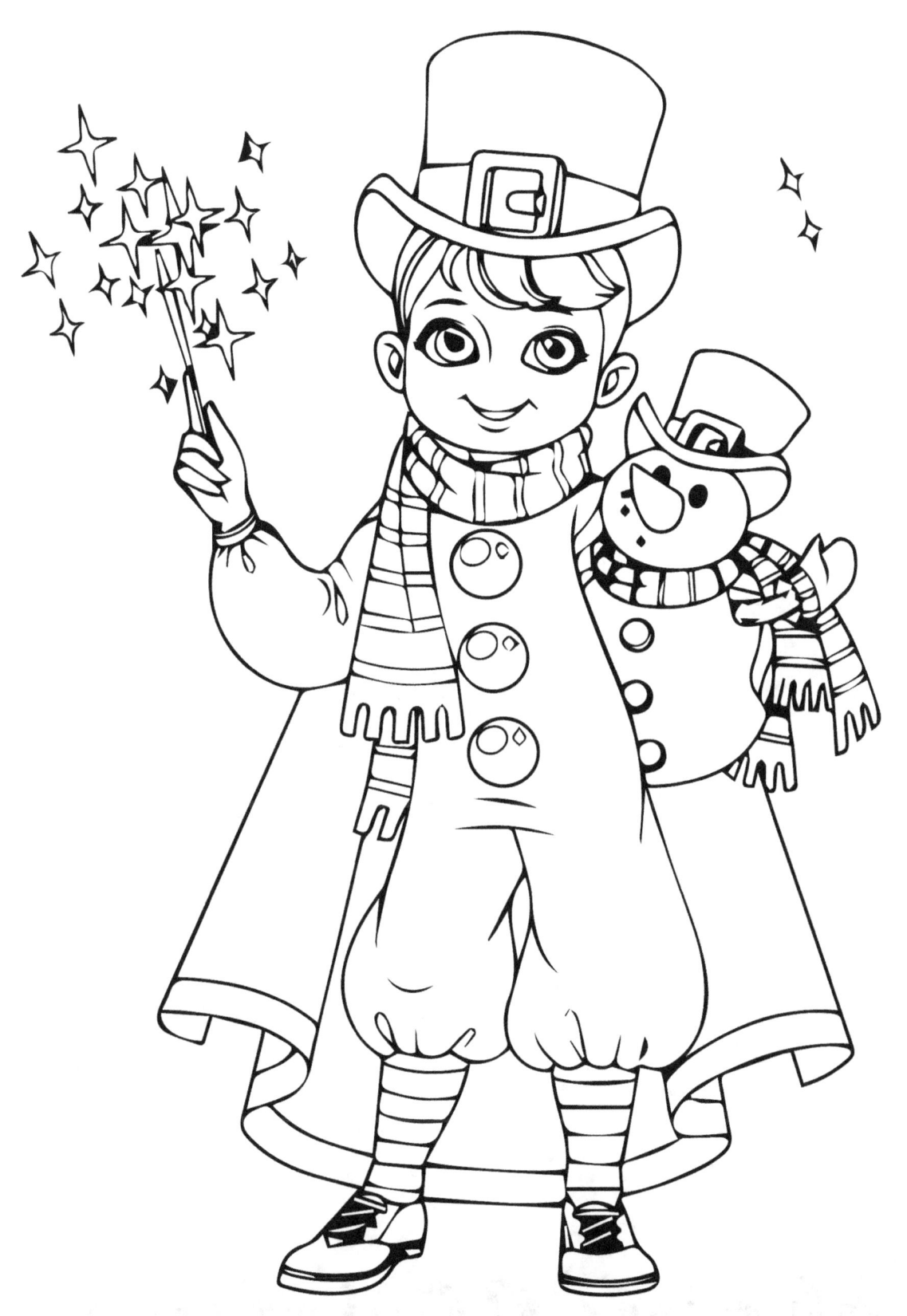

Merry Christmas

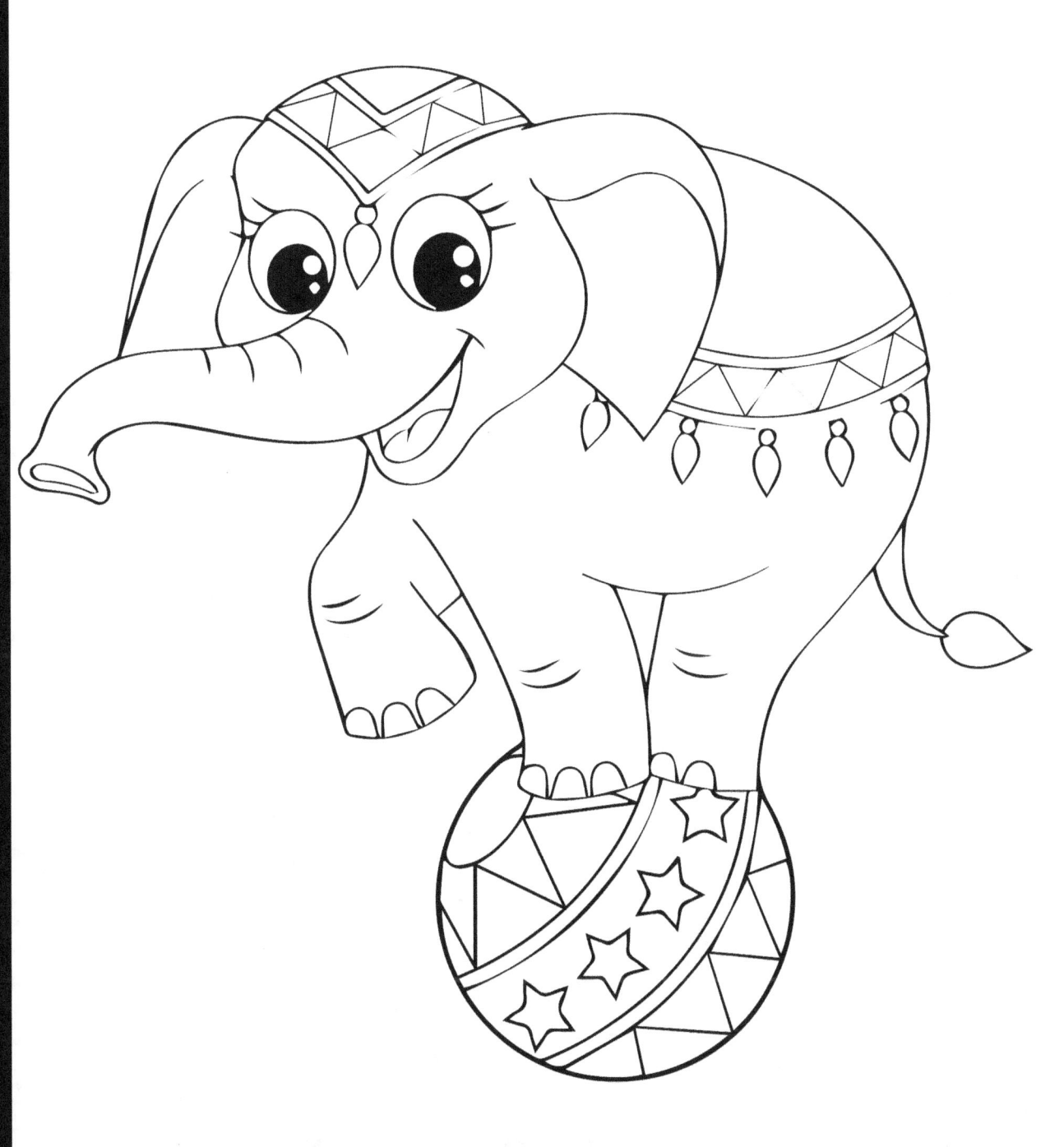

Merry Christmas

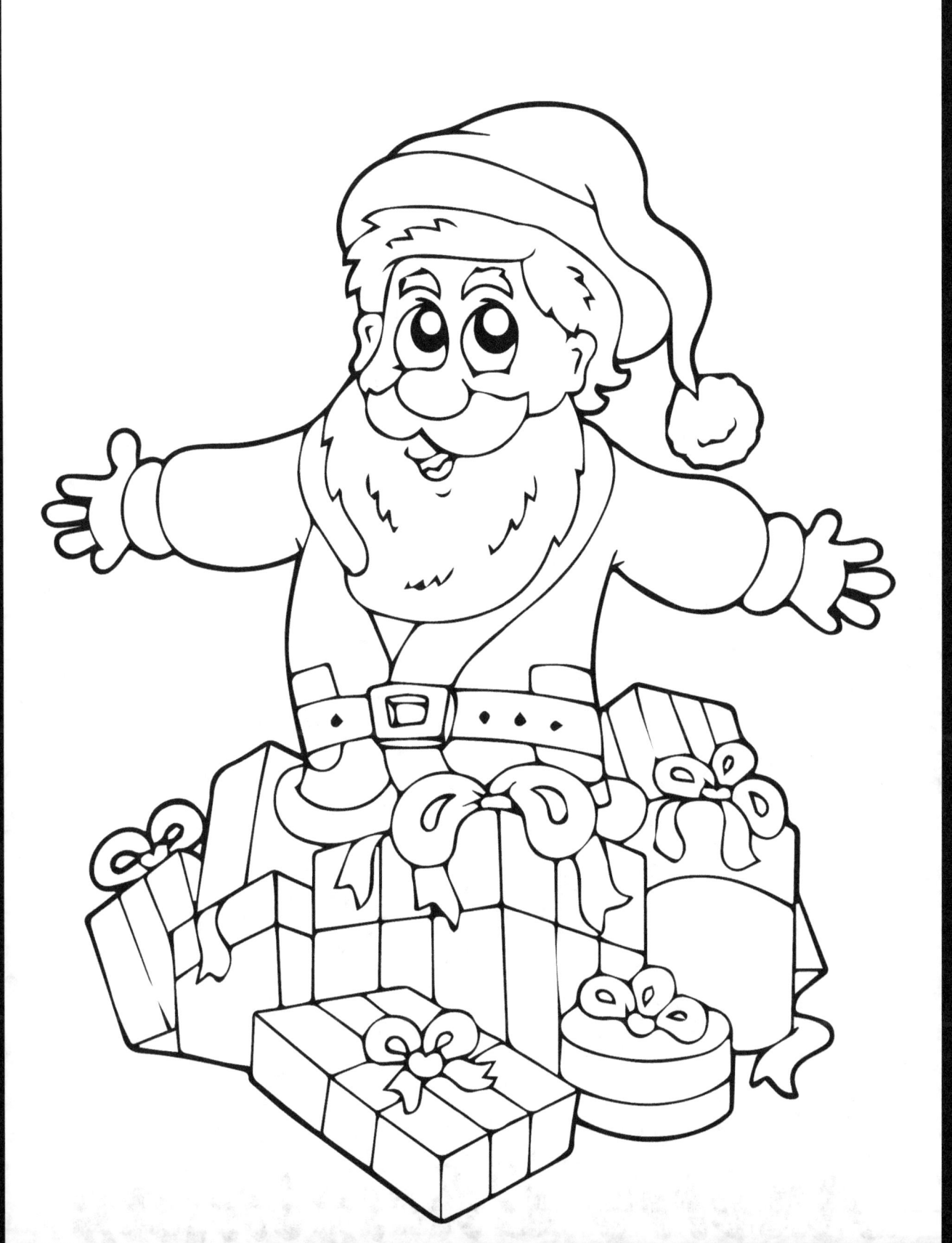

Merry Christmas

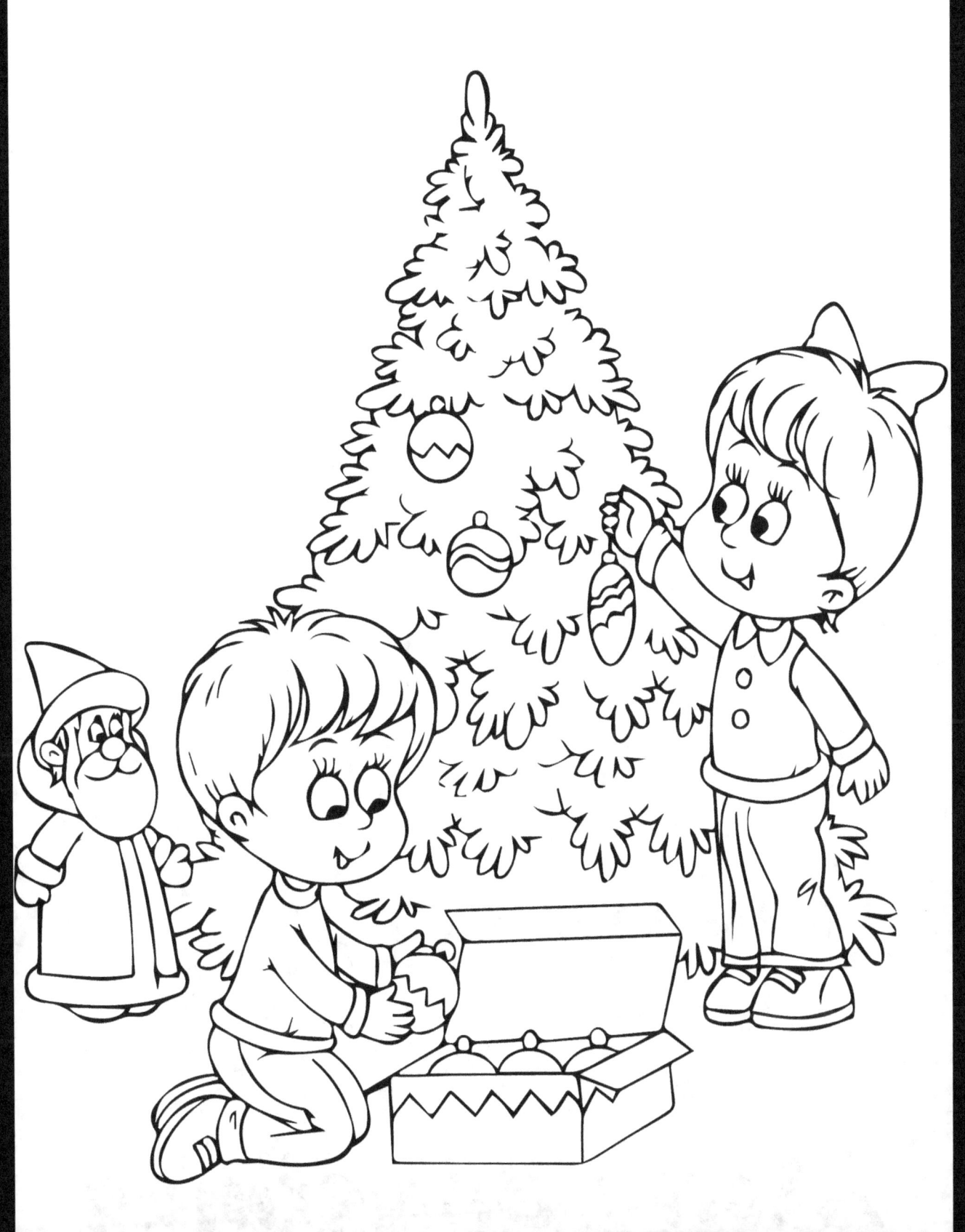

Merry Christmas

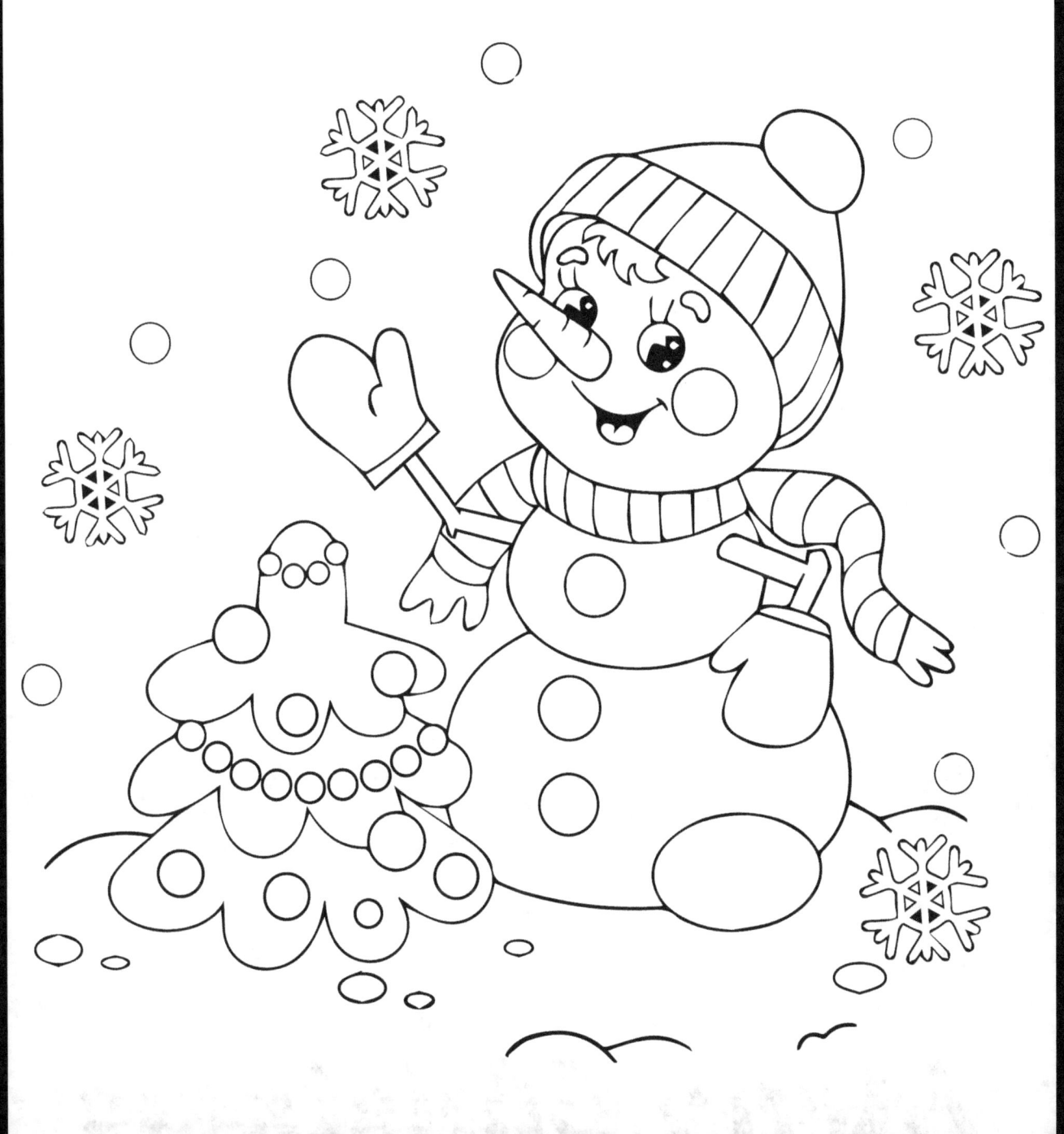

Merry Christmas

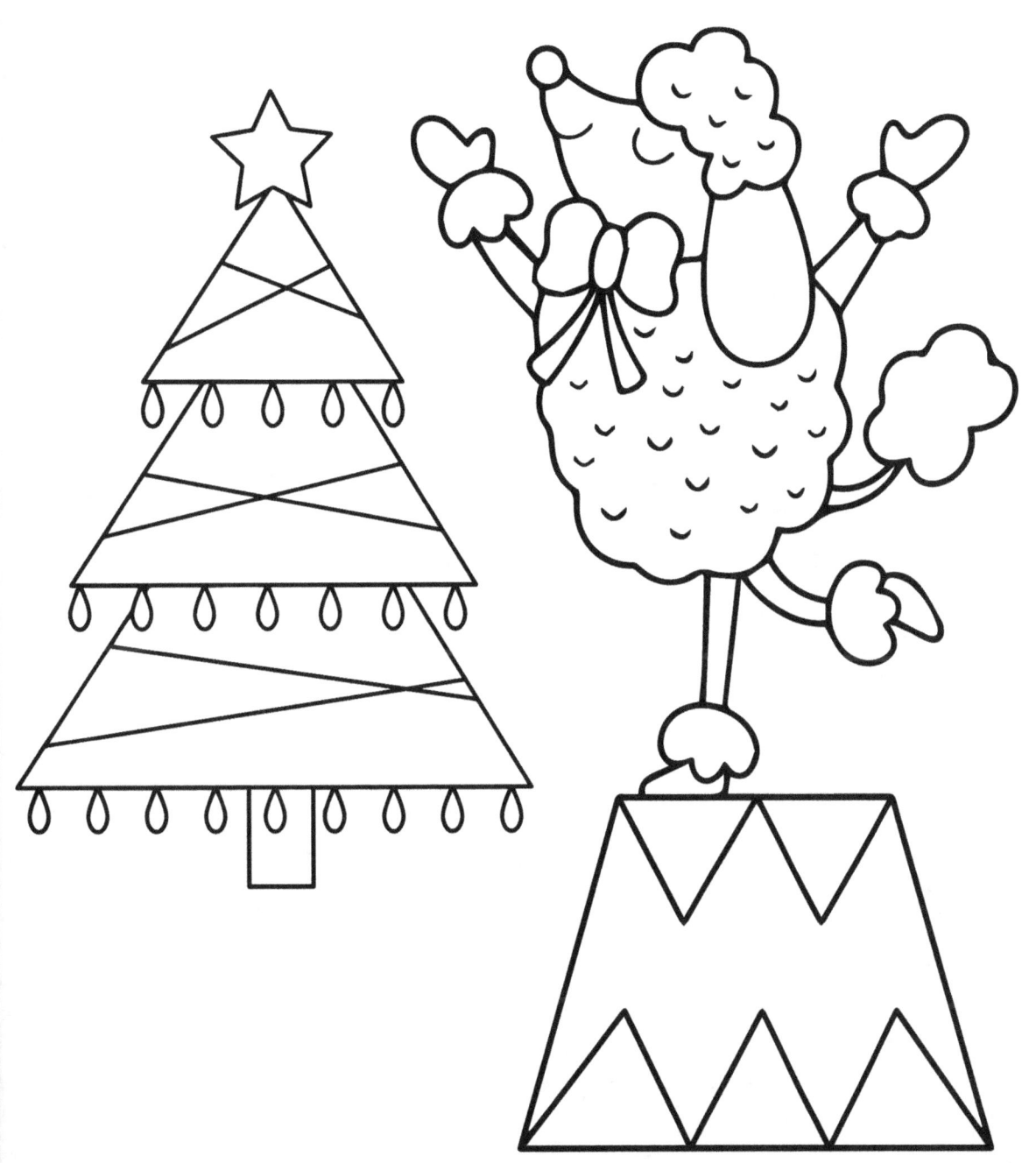

Merry Christmas

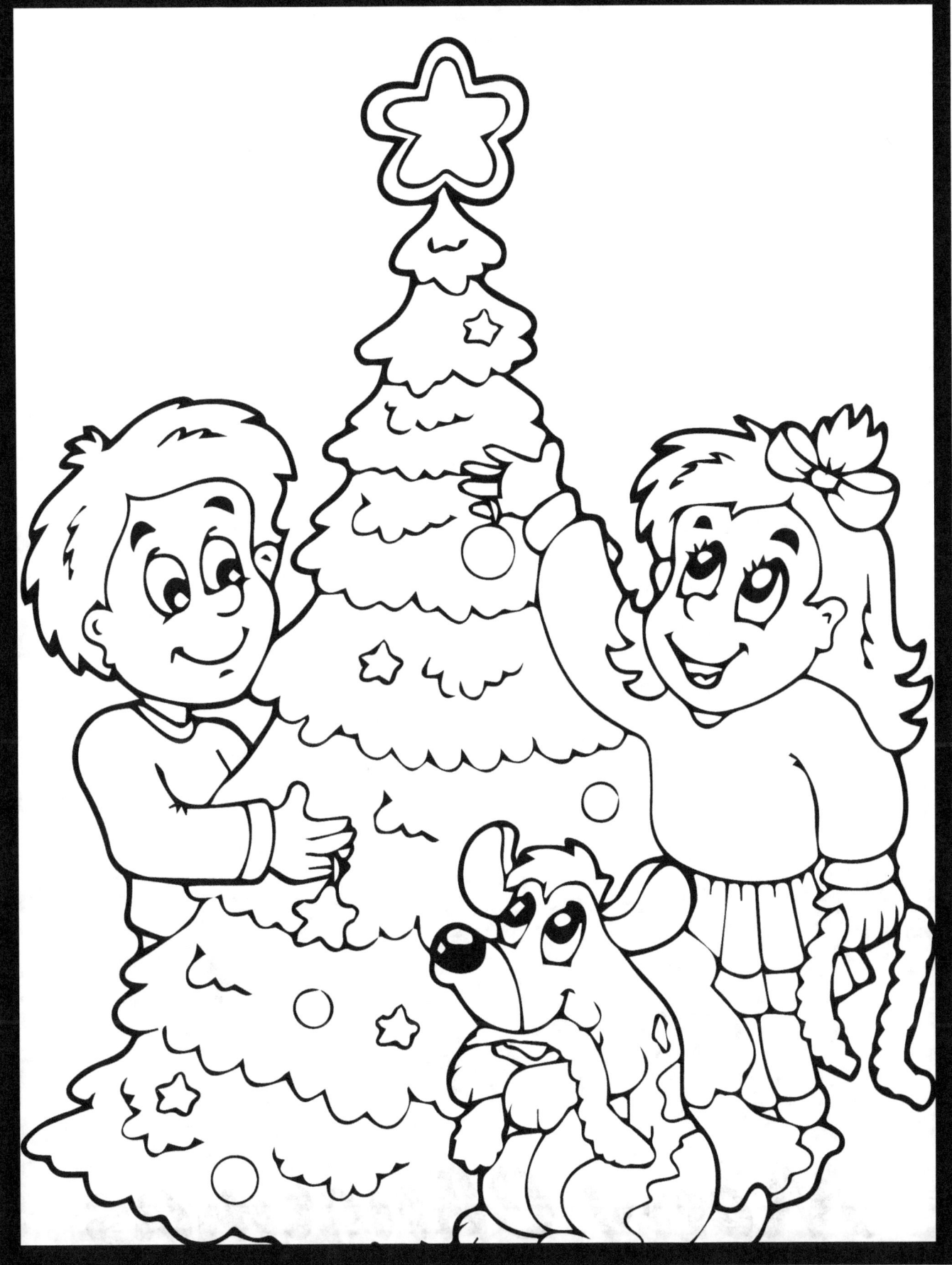

Merry Christmas

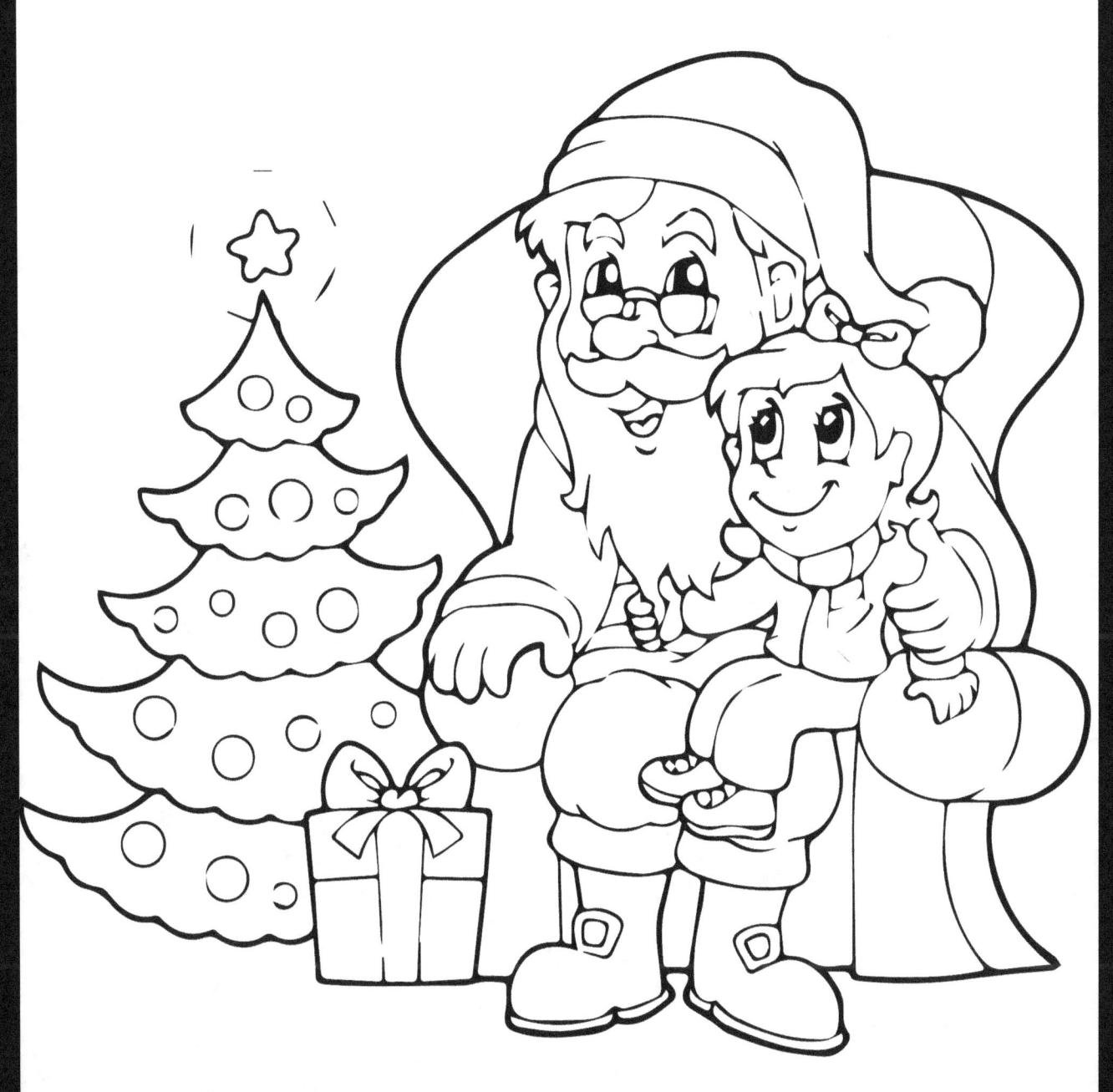

Merry Christmas

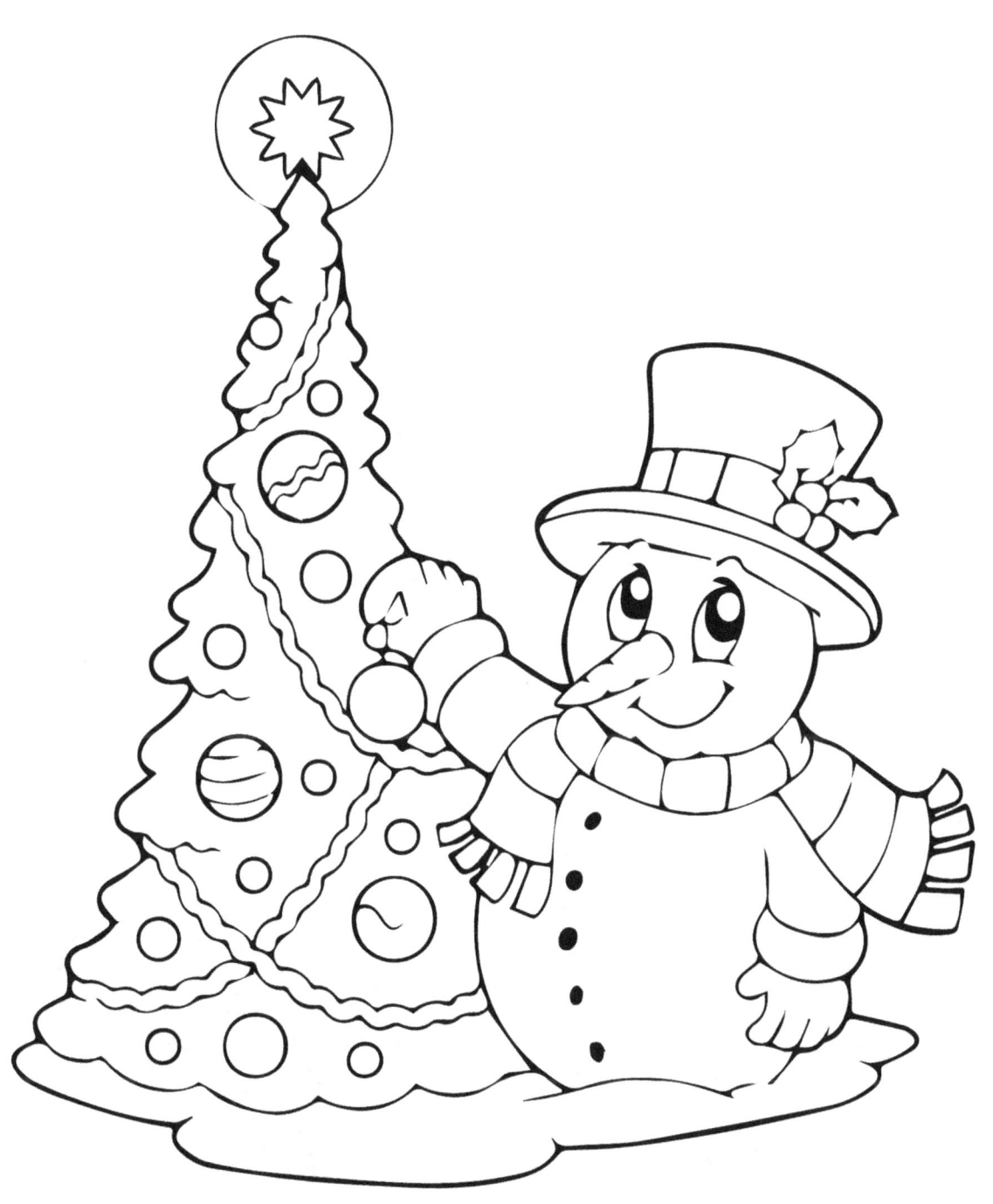

Merry Christmas

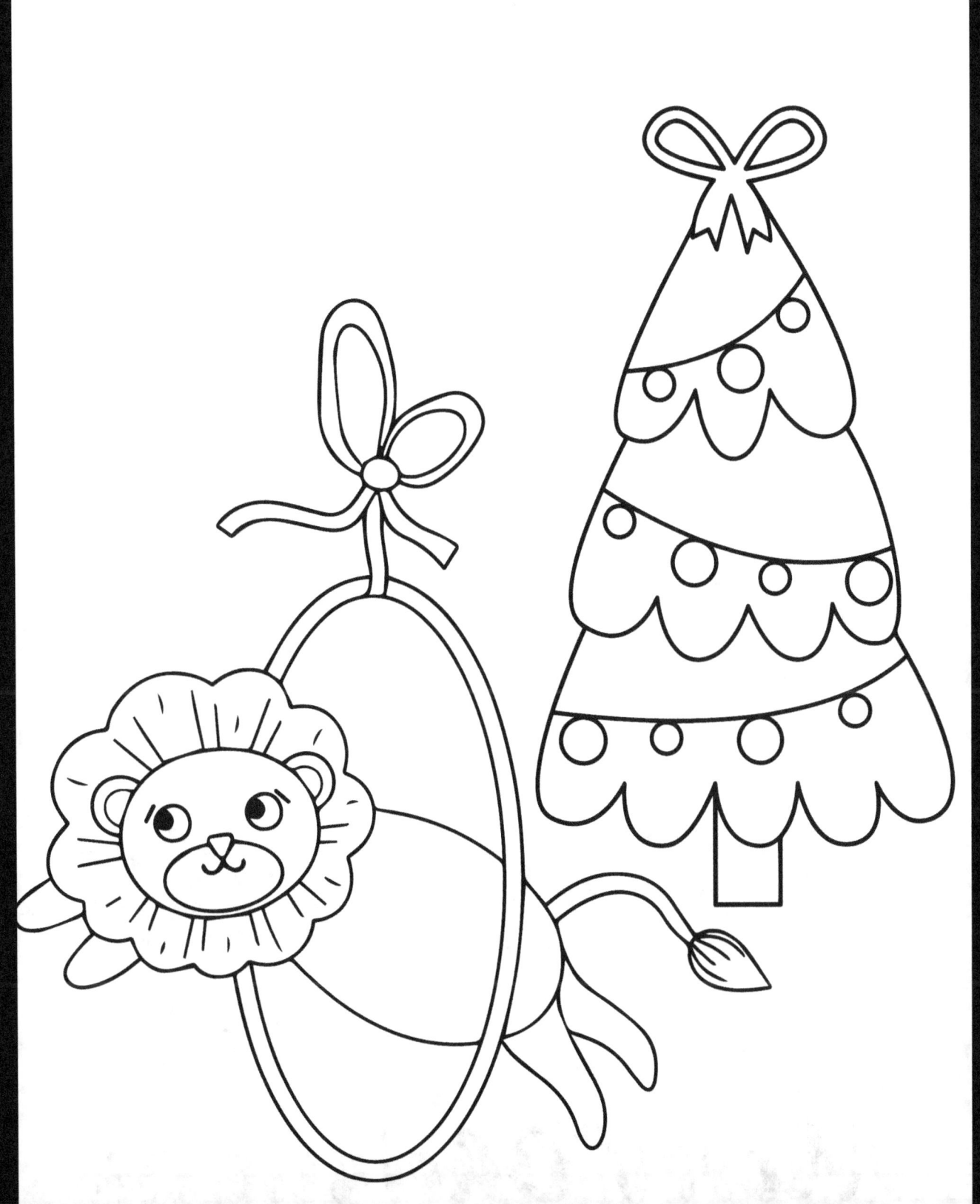

Merry Christmas

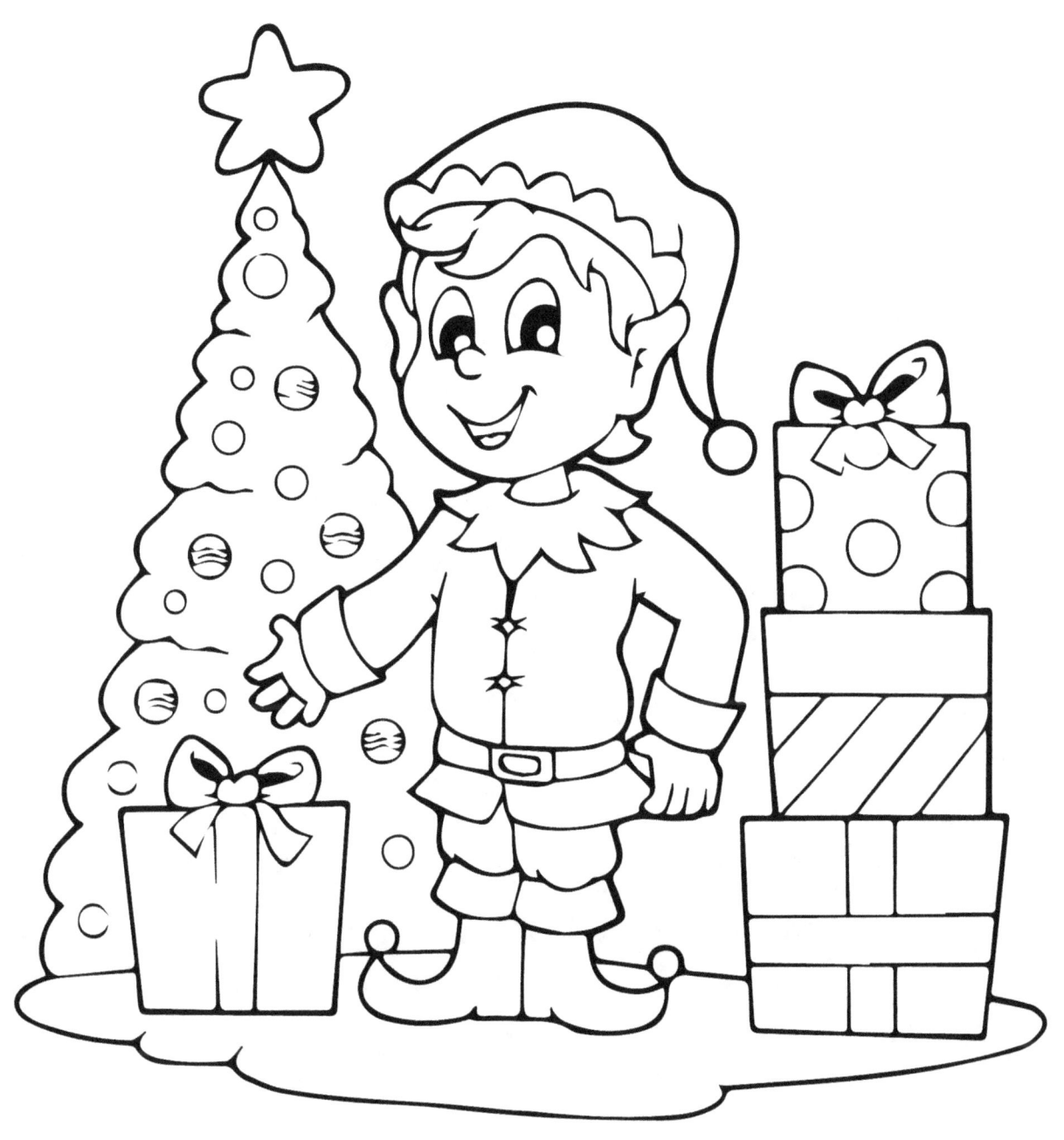

Merry Christmas

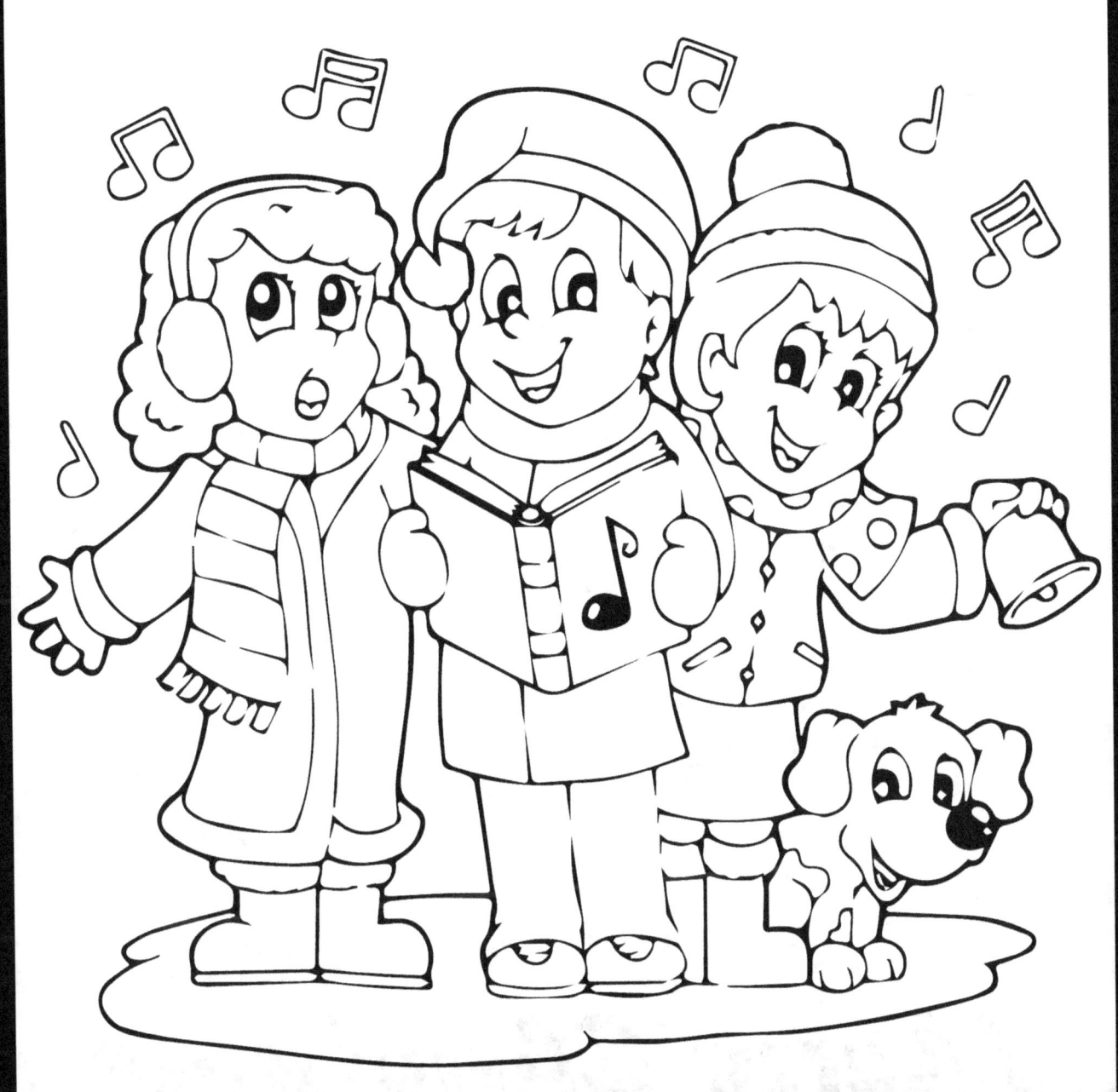

Merry Christmas

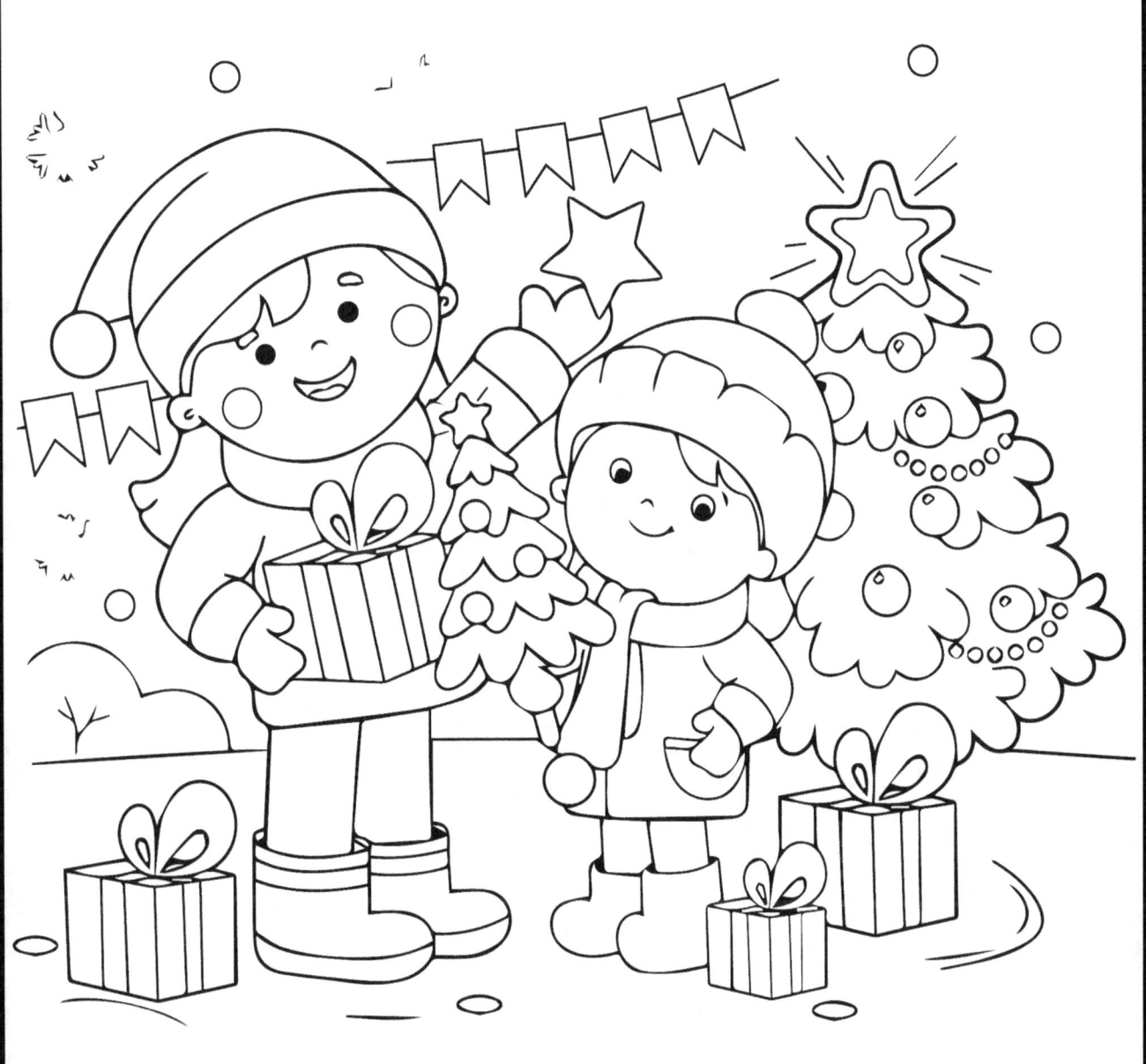

Merry Christmas

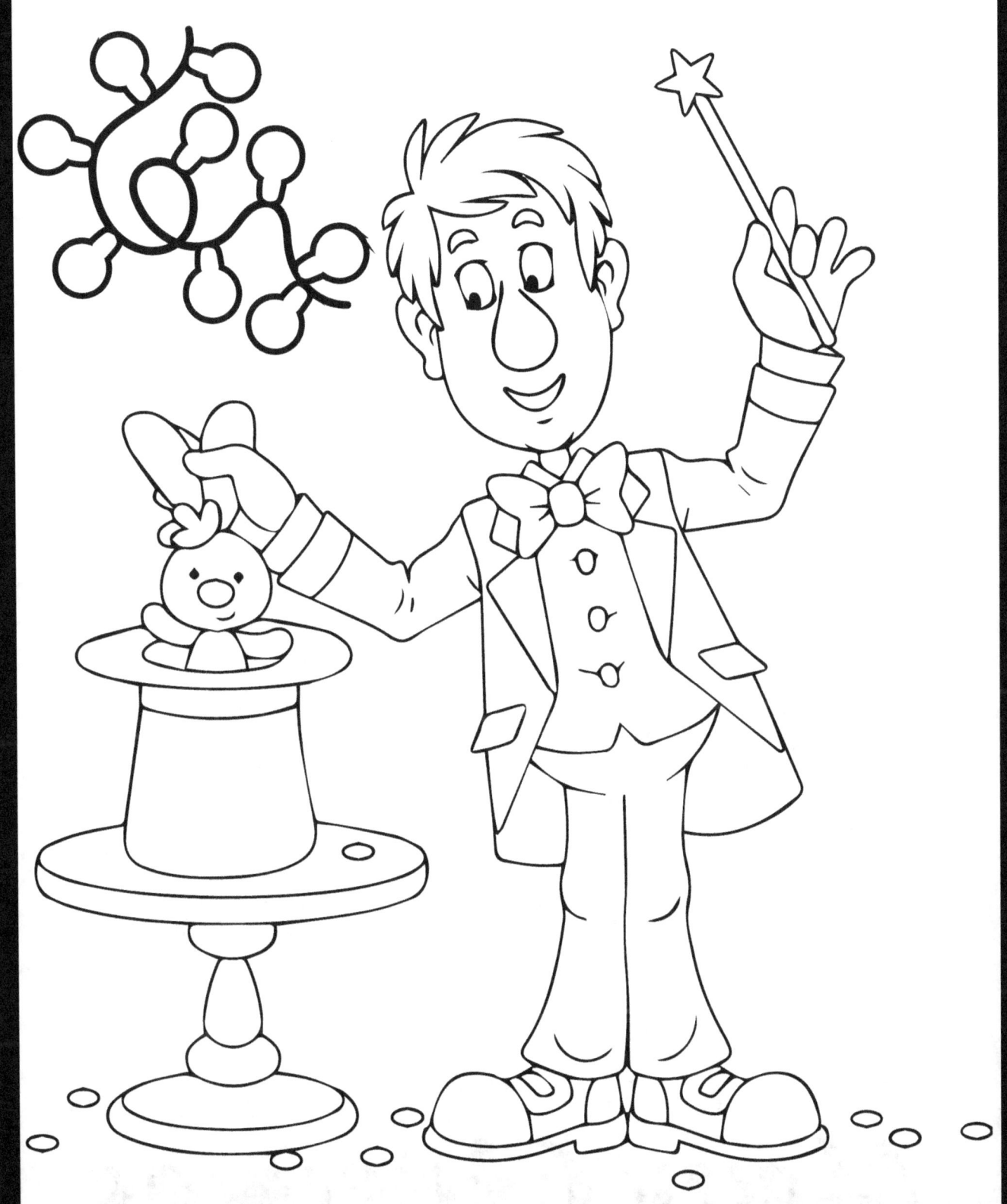

Merry Christmas

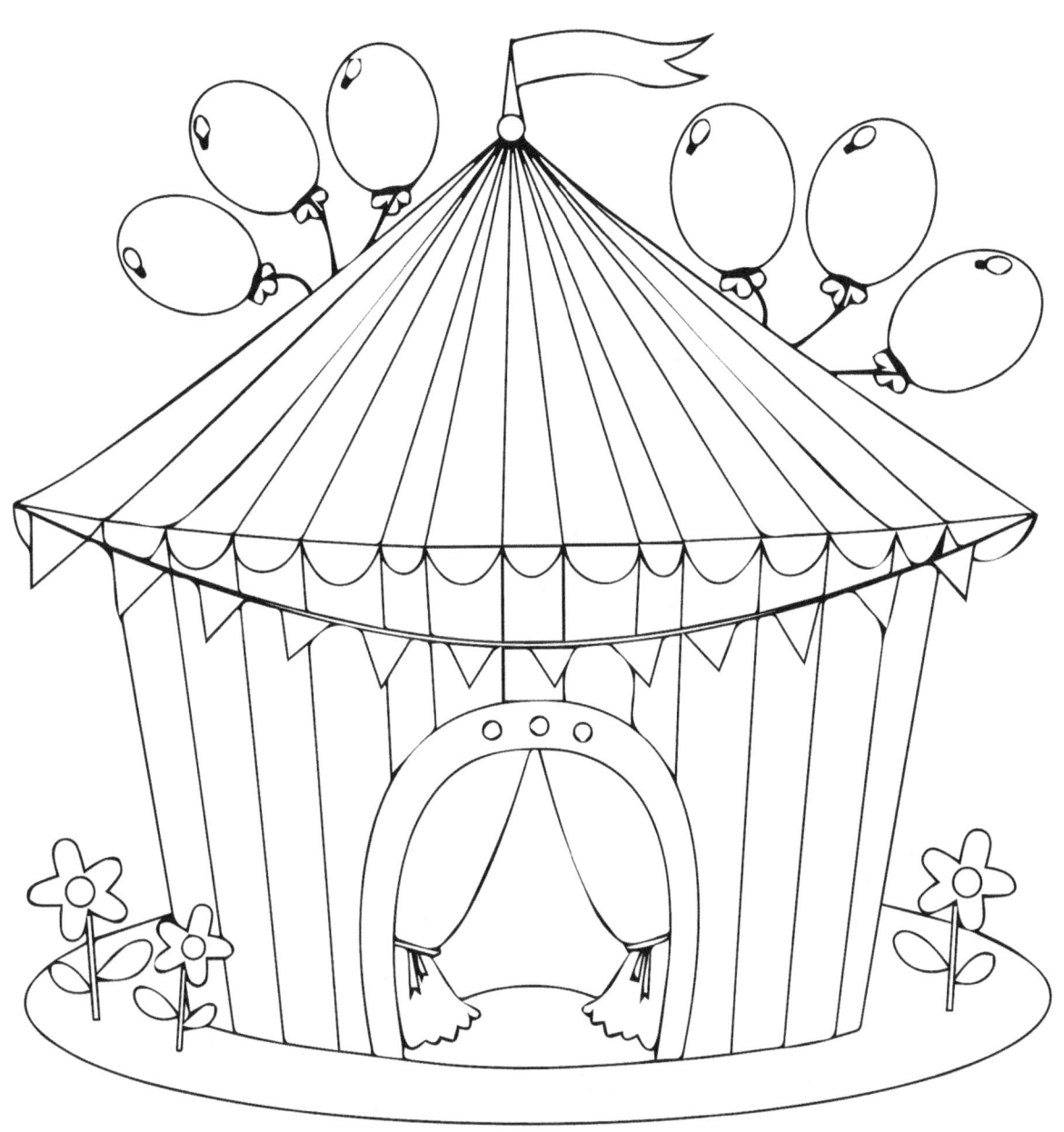

Merry Christmas

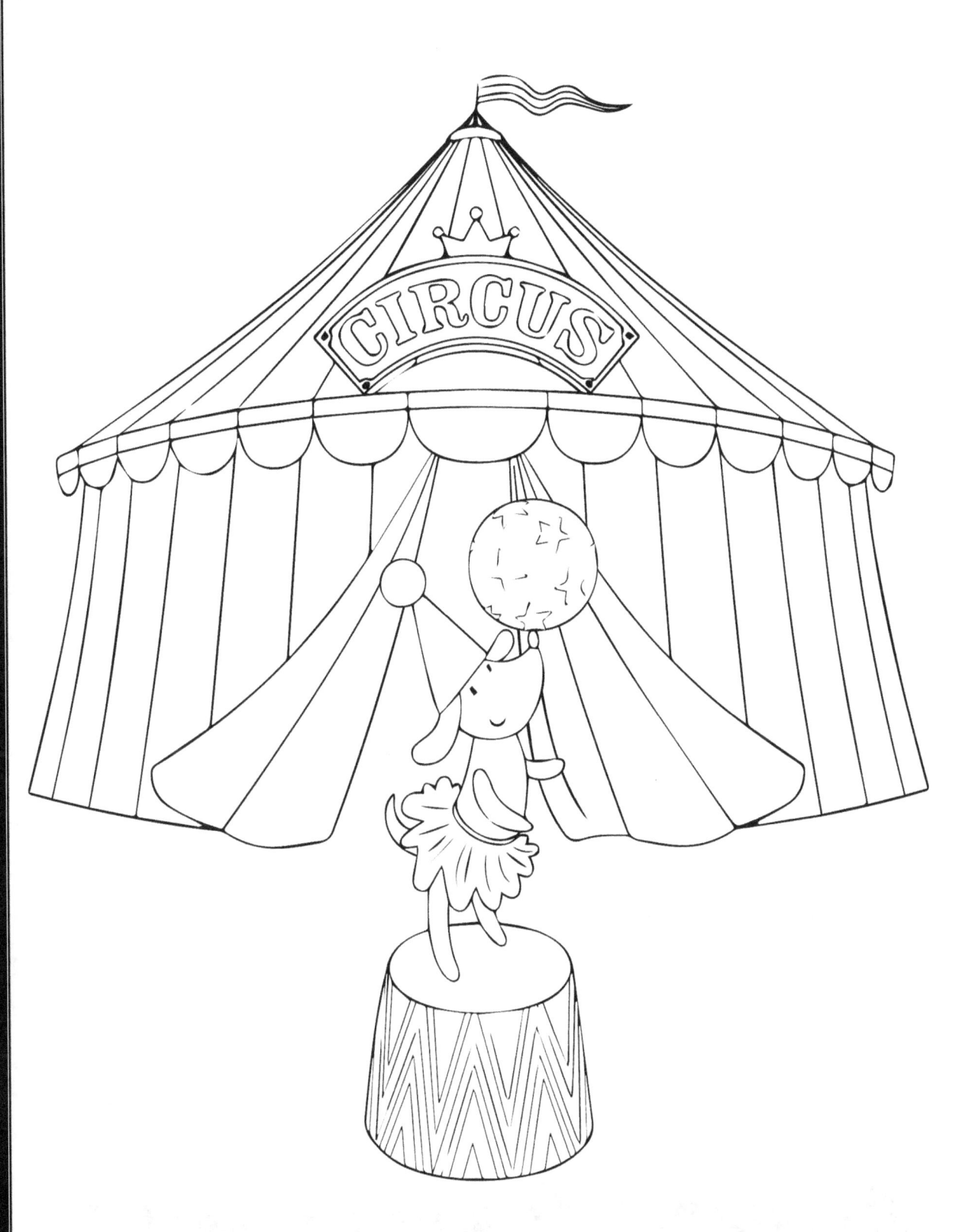

Merry Christmas

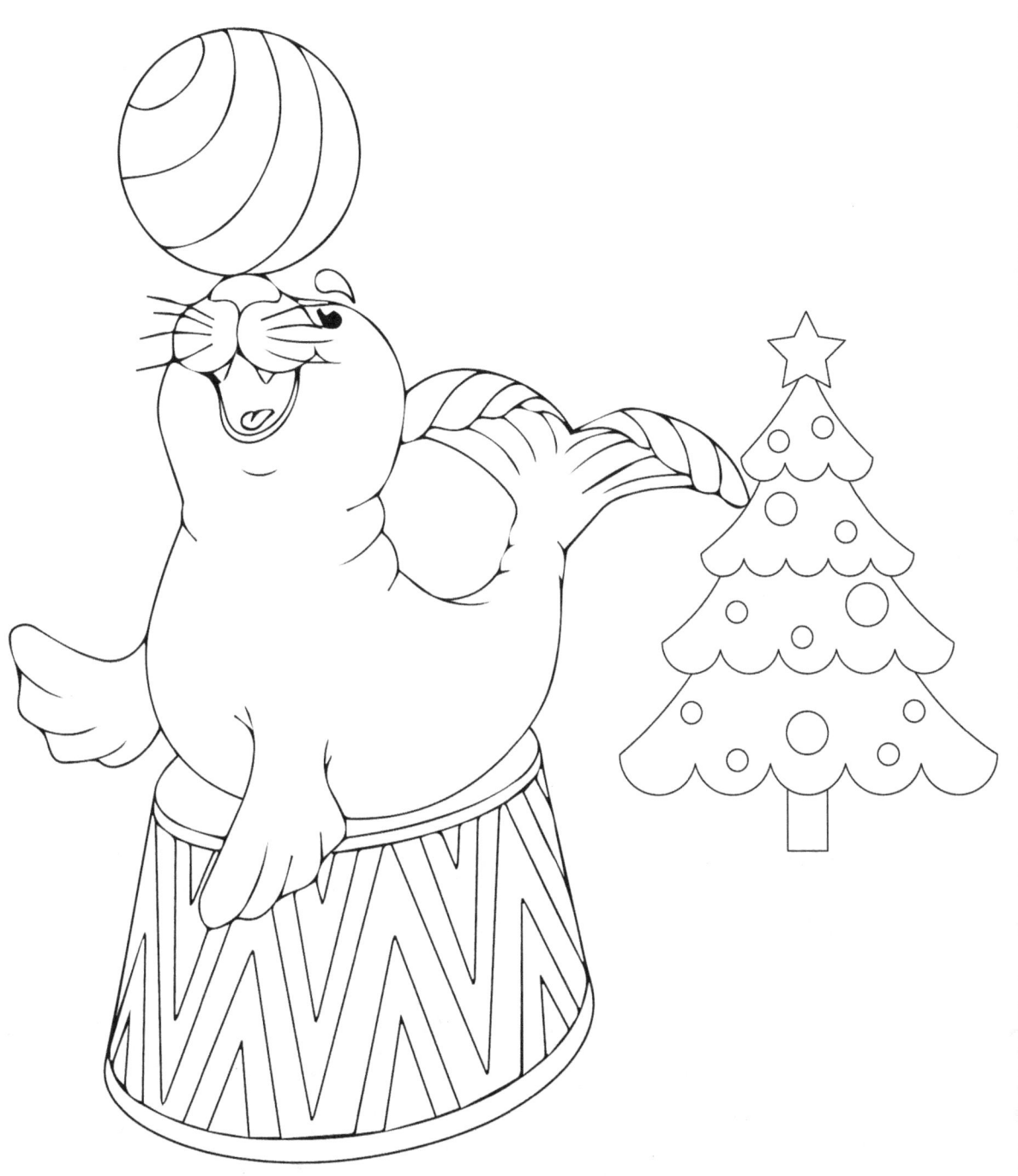

Merry Christmas

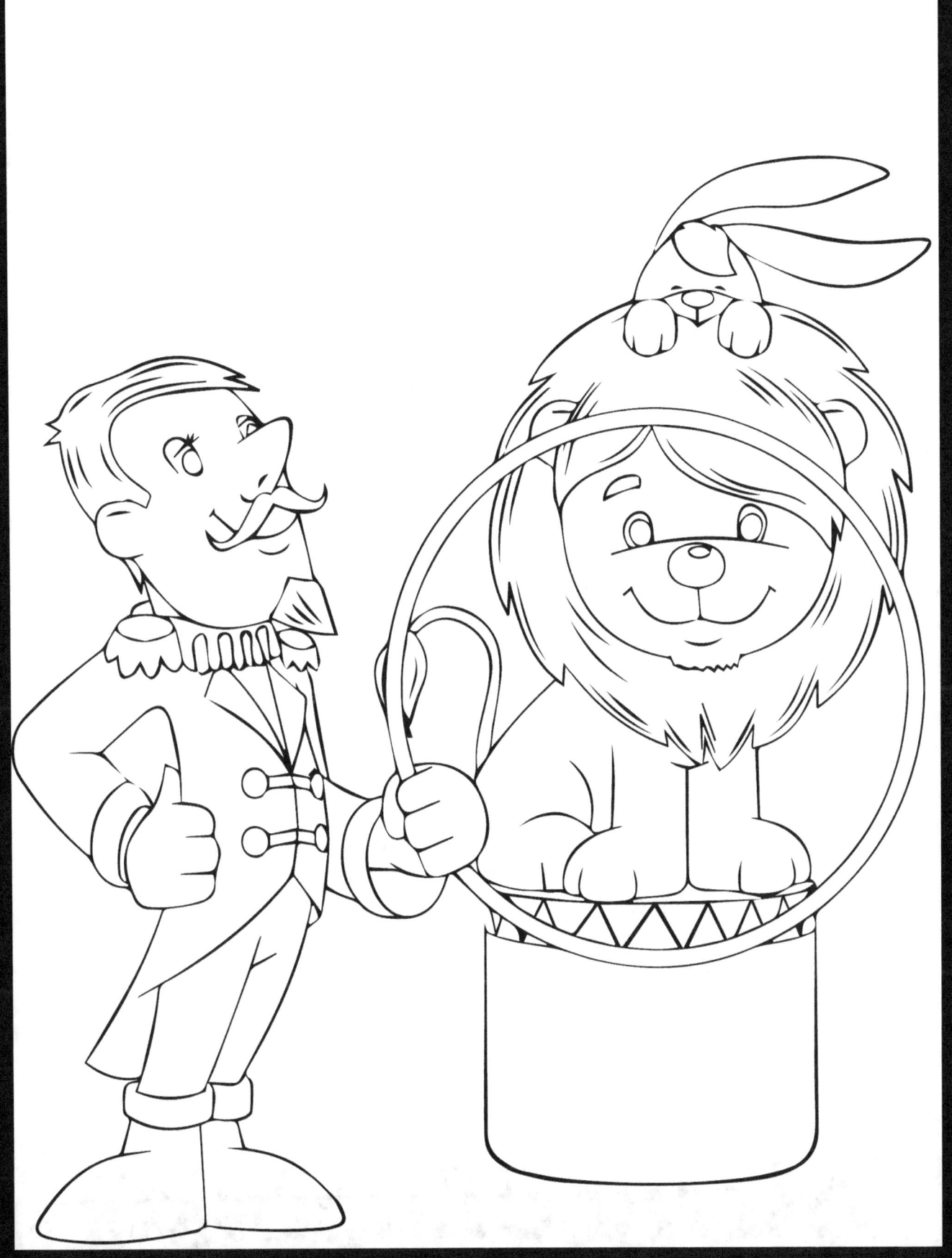

Merry Christmas

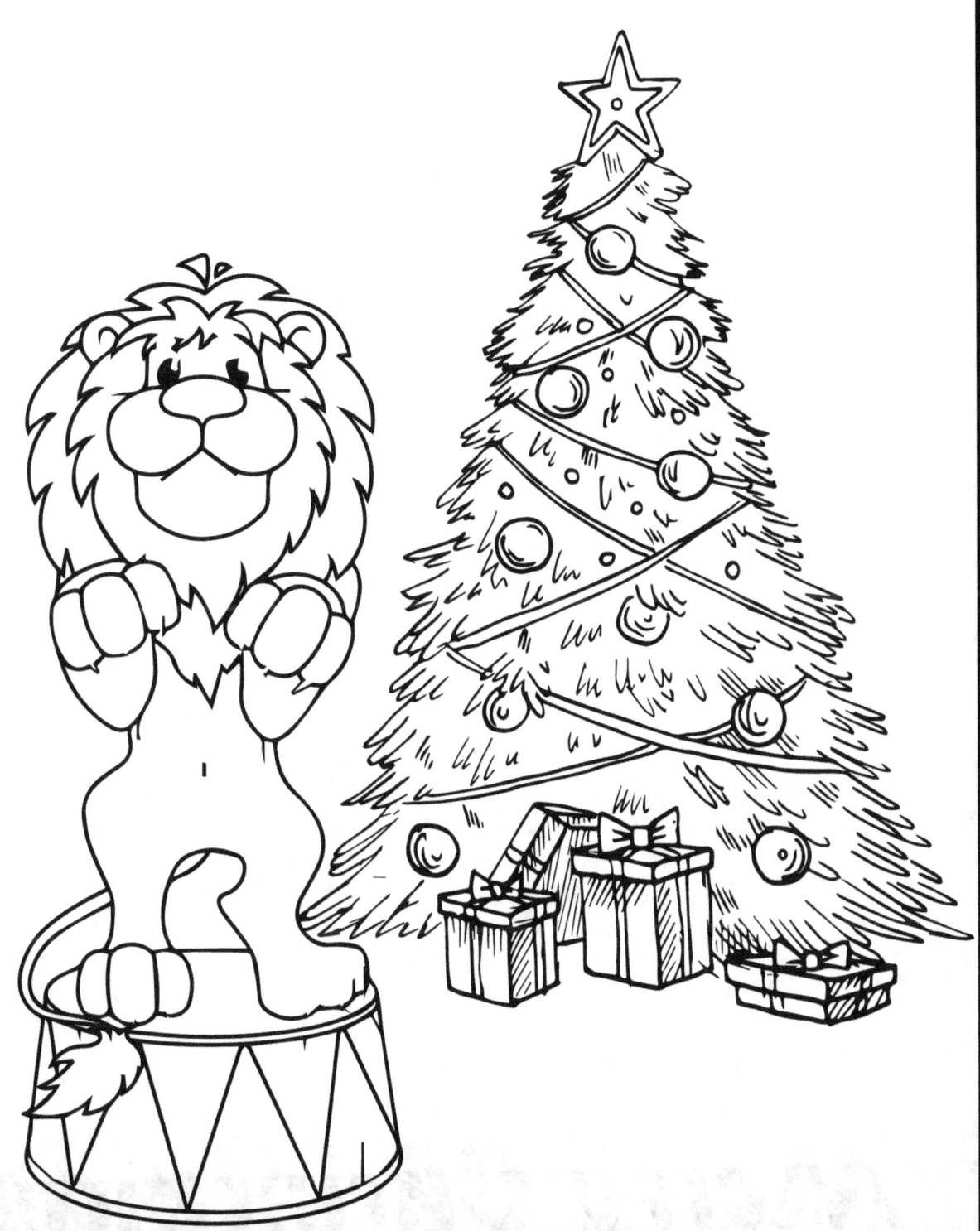

Merry Christmas

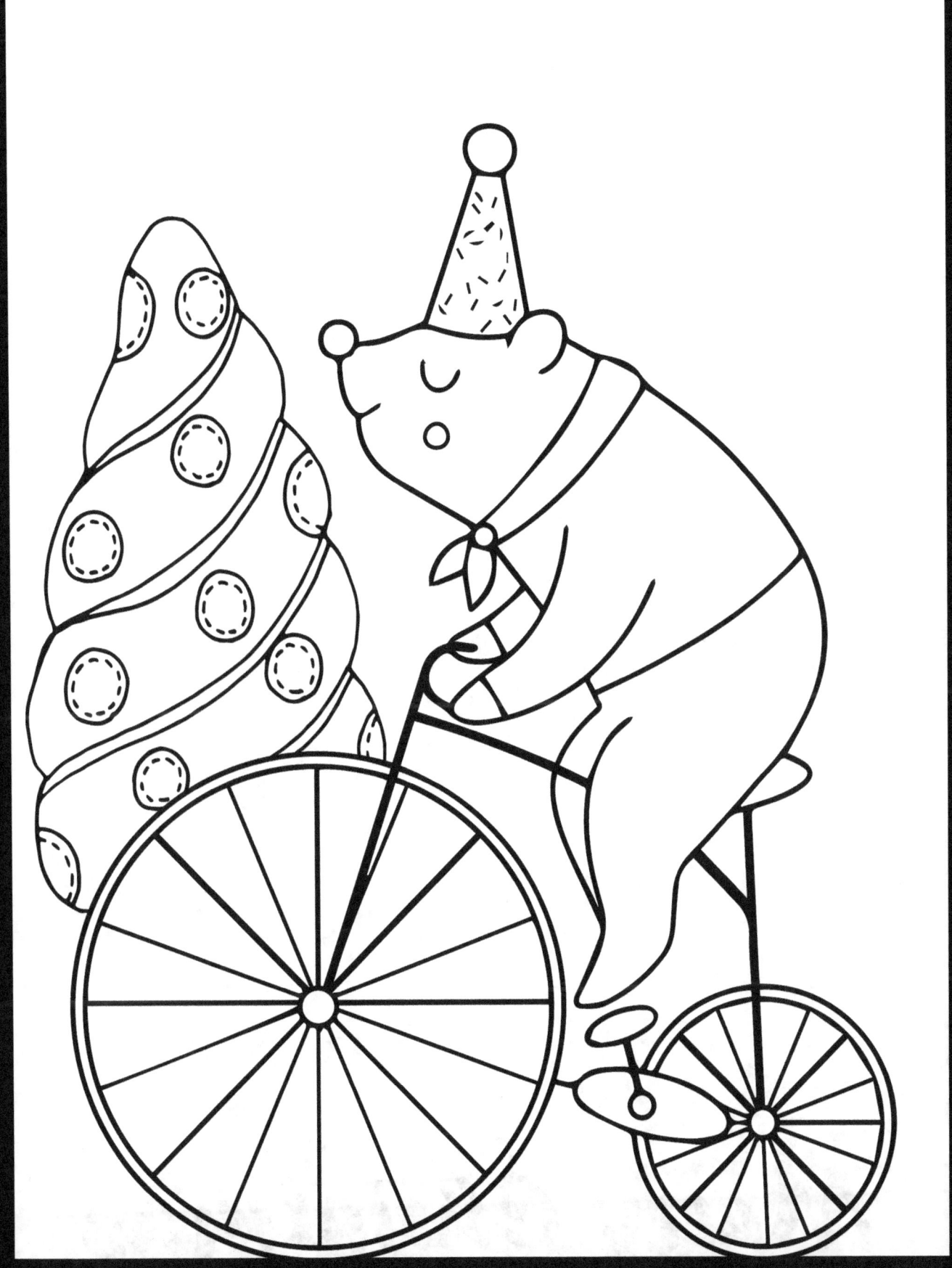

Merry Christmas

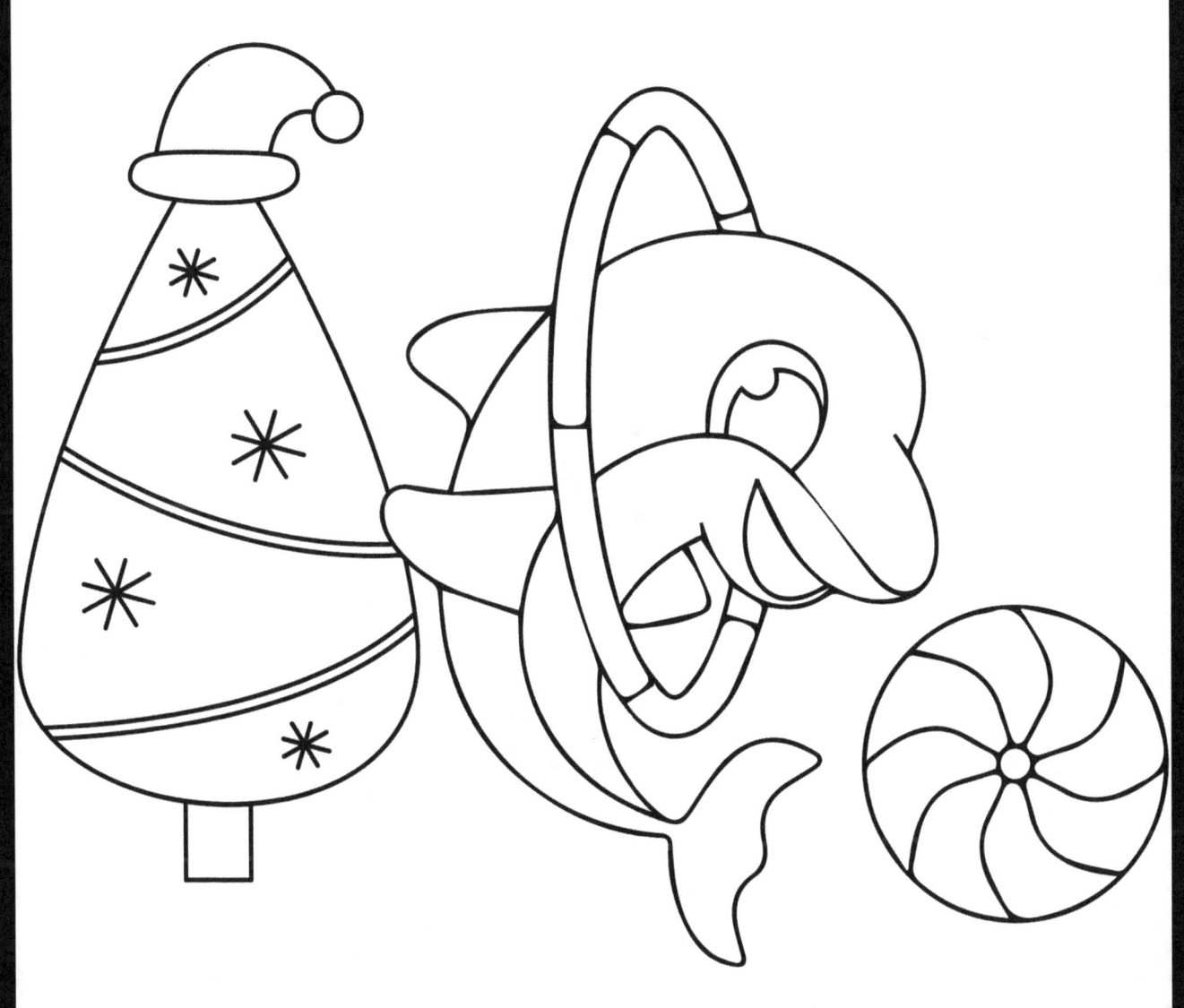

Merry Christmas

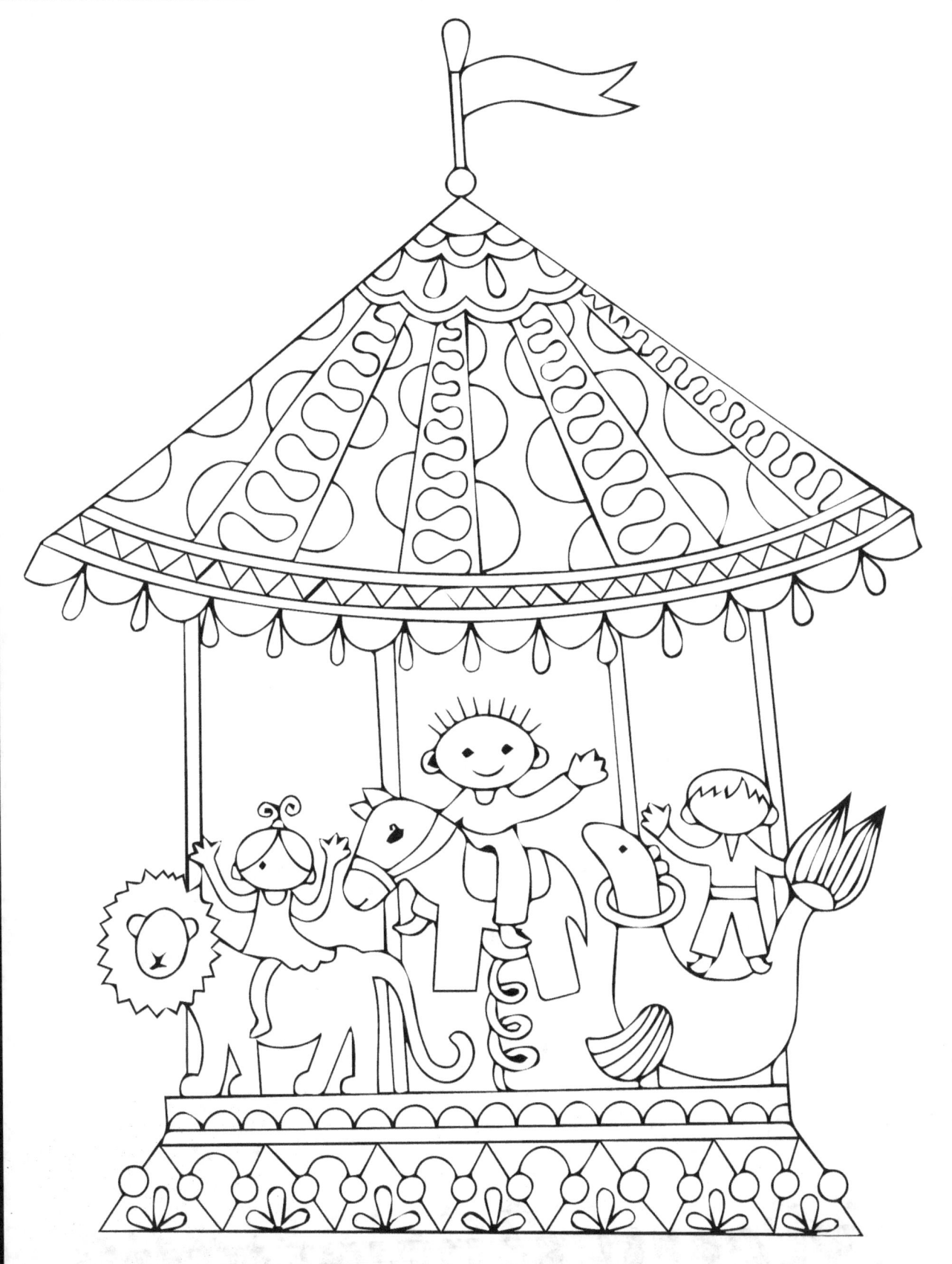

Merry Christmas

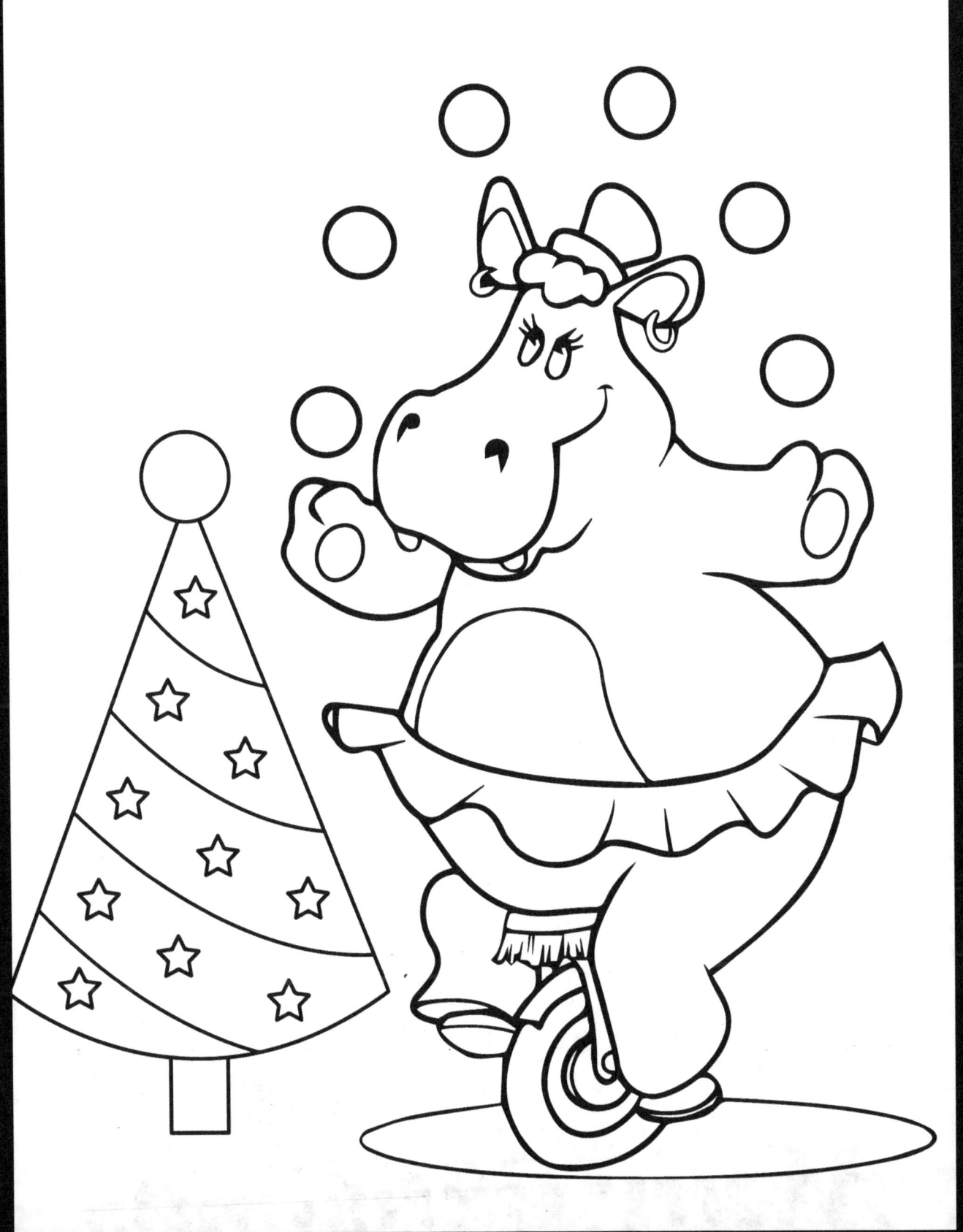

Merry Christmas

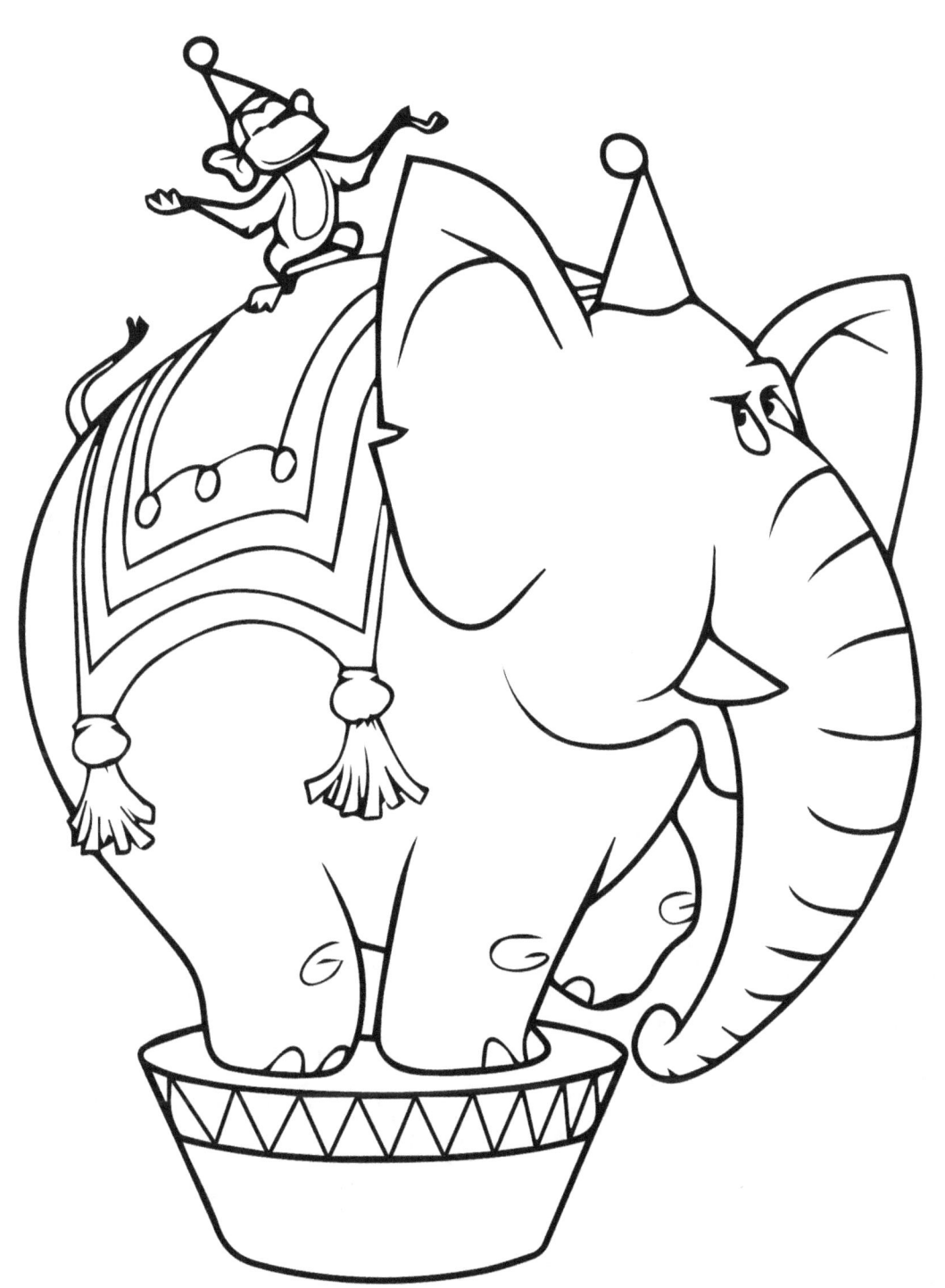

Merry Christmas